# Becoming A Consciously Aligned Leader

*An Emerging Conscious Leader's*
*Mini-Handbook*
*For Aligning with Their Next Levels*
*Of Success*

## Alicia "WATERS"

For ordering, booking, permission, or questions, contact the author.
www.anwempires@gmail.com
www.amazon.com/author/alicianwaters

ISBN-13:978-1502555571

Printed in the United States of America by Create Space

**Becoming A Consciously Aligned Leader**

## *Dedication & Acknowledgments*

This is a general dedication to every current and emerging conscious leader who is desiring to align with their greatest levels of success to impact many.

I give thanks to God and to every individual who has served as agents of change to assist with the elevation of my personal, professional and spiritual evolution as a conscious leader.

# *Table of Contents*

## Introduction

*Becoming A Consciously Aligned Leader* is a very timely read for adopting and adapting to the continued global shifts in new paradigm leadership. As our planet continues to realigned and experienced a re-birthing process, it is only natural that humanity who was formed from earth and Spirit should organically fall under the same order.

This work is designed to be a divine catalyst to induce change and awareness for our world to begin realigning with our primary core values. This journey of connecting back to our truth begins with revolutionizing leaders, who will choose the path of conscious evolution.

The new era of conscious leadership will represent the true essence of a new evolving paradigm so that they can demonstrate this expression to those whom they will impact.

**Becoming A Consciously Aligned Leader**

The primary goal of this read is to assist leaders in becoming more spiritually and consciously aligned with their divine design through holistic self-mastery. The key foundational areas involve an up-level in personal-mastery, divine shifts, and proper alignments. These core areas help to elevate consciousness for achieving a high level of self-mastery.

I invite every leader and emerging leader to embrace this book as a guide to help accomplish holistic self-mastery and divine alignments, so that as often as possible, they will live the life that they were meant to live.

Through becoming more consciously aligned, you will begin to experience greater success in your personal, professional and spiritual journey. This can always be accomplished if you elevate your consciousness and begin looking inward for the growth, change and solutions that you desire to see.

**Becoming A Consciously Aligned Leader**

# *Becoming A Consciously Aligned Leader*

For the last several years I have been on an inner quest for discovering and awakening to more of my divine purpose and personal truth. This has consisted of a ten-year journey process of successes, betrayals, trials, and errors while doing the inner-work to establish self-mastery.

This has also been a journey of integrating higher states of consciousness for greater awareness of connecting deeper with the Spirit, in order to come into greater alignment with the core essence of my being.

Throughout my experiences of having certain levels of success, transitions, and reinventions, I've come to know the importance of living from your true authentic place along with being conscious as I continue my personal mastery adventure.

**Becoming A Consciously Aligned Leader**

One of my divine callings is to help establish better global leadership. Over the last fifteen years of serving in leadership roles in areas such as ministry, hotel management, leadership trainer-coach, high-level service professional and as a current business owner, I've experienced and witnessed the good, bad and ugly sides of leadership.

I have observed my own strengths and fallacies and also those of many who have been in leadership with me, both locally and globally. Each, dealing with the same insecurities, egos, competitiveness, self-absorbedness and fighting about our differences when we are all more alike than we are different. It makes you wonder why our world appears to be in such a dysfunctional state.

As leaders, when we lead from the place of spiritual misalignment along with a lack of understanding of who we were created to be, we transfer that same

**Becoming A Consciously Aligned Leader**

spirit to those whom we desire to impact and in turn they will more than likely go and imitate those patterns.

One of my primary goals in my leadership endeavors is to ensure that leaders and people of great influence align with their personal, professional and spiritual paths so that they don't fall into the same types of patterns that we've seen in our history, which have not reflected the greater plan of God for humanities evolution.

My challenge for higher consciousness and personal mastery is first to those who are in current leadership roles and next to new emerging leaders as they embark on the journey.

The consciously aligned leader of this era must know how to make the proper adjustments and become masterful for achieving holistic success.

**Becoming A Consciously Aligned Leader**

Leaders must become more awake by using all of the aspects of everyday life to be their universities for discovering how to show up in their truth. Establishing higher levels of consciousness and awareness creates the greater alignments for their purpose and destiny.

Over the years, I've observed and experienced for myself the lack of authentic alignment with Spirit, that we as leaders can fall into, especially in business and ministry. Leaders will become so caught up in doing the work of the Spirit that they forget about truly communing with the Spirit of the work.

Often, most spend so much time trying to accomplish fulfilling their divine callings in their own will-power. Neglecting to access their divinity within. Most, often miss the opportunities to allow Spirit to infuse everything situation to make endeavors flow with more grace and ease.

**Becoming A Consciously Aligned Leader**

Our misalignments cause us to overwork ourselves and neglect proper self-care by having too many irons in the fire; thinking that we have to act on every great idea that hits our minds. Sometimes we don't realize that everything is not ours to do or it's not always the time to bring it to fruition.

I've witnessed several leaders from different industries allow their health and financial areas to decline based on over-managing the details and failing to use proper delegation.

Several, are always wanting to be in total control along with using a lack of good discernment when it comes to making the right investments of time or money.

As leaders and people of great influence become more consciously aligned with their purpose, they'll come into greater awareness that the world is watching and

**Becoming A Consciously Aligned Leader**

depending on leadership to represent examples of divine wholeness.

It's not that we have to be perfect, yet our chief aim should be to strive to achieve the highest level of our soul's evolution so that this reflection invites others to join in on this journey of mastering themselves.

There are two quotes, one by author John Foster and the other by Dee Hock, founder of *Visa International*, that really stand out to me concerning the reasons why it is important to master your inner game as a leader for making a greater impact.

These two quotes speak to the very heart of why personal mastery for leadership is the pivotal shift that is needed in today's world:

**Becoming A Consciously Aligned Leader**

*"A man without decision of character can never be said to belong to himself . . . . He belongs to whatever can make captive of him."*

*~Author John Foster*

*"Control is not leadership; management is not leadership; leadership is leadership is leadership. If you seek to lead, invest at least 50% of your time leading yourself—your own purpose, ethics, principles, motivation, conduct. Invest at least 20% leading those with authority over you and 15% leading your peers.*

*If you don't understand that you work for your mislabeled 'subordinates,' then you know nothing of leadership. You know only tyranny."*

*~ Dee Hock*

*Founder and CEO Emeritus*

*VISA International*

**Becoming A Consciously Aligned Leader**

As leaders, if we are not leading from a healthy disposition, then we will continue to witness even the best of influential people fall down in the areas of integrity, being egotistical and having abusive controlling systems that impact the world in very negative ways.

**Becoming A Consciously Aligned Leader**

## *Make the Proper Life & Mindset Shifts*

If you're not familiar with Feng Shui, it is an ancient and wise approach to the way we are affected by our surrounding environment. Feng Shui helps individuals learn how to properly organize and rearrange their surroundings to improve the balance and overall quality of life.

This process normally involves the harmonization of the environment using the five elements which are water, wood, fire, earth, and metal. Each element has its own function within the environment.

We are able to do the same thing with a process from within that I call, "Your Internal Feng Shui Shift." This allows us to master our inner game by using our intuition, the elements and the guidance of the Spirit.

**Becoming A Consciously Aligned Leader**

These key components are available 24 hours a day to assist us with what we need to release or shift inwardly. Your outside environment is just a reflection of you and your relationship with the universe. However, I believe we each have the power to realign our inner conditions which will eventually result in seeing a change in our outward circumstance.

You will eventually become your own Avatar or the last air-bender of your own inner stewardship. This inner realignment will reflect back in your outer alignment.

**Becoming A Consciously Aligned Leader**

# *4 Internal Shifts Required for*

# *Aligning You for Achieving External Success*

1. **Shift Your Perspective -** Having the willingness to be open to change when it comes to your situations.

2. **Shift and Re-position Your Point of View -** Being open to adopting and adapting to a New Paradigm to advance your overall success and well-being.

3. **Shift in Mindset -** Often we need a shift in our mindset, which involves our perspective and inner spirit in order to become realigned for accomplishing our next steps.

4. **Shift from Organizing Your Life to Aligning It-** Becoming more congruent with your path is more important than establishing order in the beginning.

**Becoming A Consciously Aligned Leader**

# A Life Aligned is A Life Divine

Alignment is one of the most critical components to divine living. A great majority of people aren't even aware of how important it is to establish divine alignments. The word alignment typically means to adjust or to produce a proper orientation. It can also mean to arrange or be arranged in a straight line.

I created a slogan several years ago, called "a life aligned is a life divine." I used this slogan to keep myself in order when I observe the flow of my work and personal affairs. If I'm trying to make something happen and it does not have an organic flow to it, then I know that I have to make a shift and realign with my personal integrity to my mission.

**Becoming A Consciously Aligned Leader**

An automobile can have the right oil change, good brakes and even new tires, however, if the alignment it off, there is going to be constantly shifting in the steering.

If the alignment is off it can cause all of the other components or well-functioning aspects of your vehicle to have problems. This is also true with organization vs. alignment as mentioned in an earlier chapter. You can have perfect order but without truly being aligned with your endeavors, can make the process very hard. The goal of allowing divine flow to occur to bring about the divine order.

Dr. Mark Chironna, Pastor of The Master's Touch International Church in Orlando Florida; in his teaching series called *Destiny & the Law of Spontaneous Desire*, he explains the importance of alignment and how we can assess our personal compass to point to our true north through identifying our six core values.

**Becoming A Consciously Aligned Leader**

I use these six core values in my *"Life Compass Alignment System"* that I've taught in a tele-class called *Life Aligned*, which helps individuals discover what their seasonal alignment is for this phase of their journey.

## Life Compass Alignment System

### (Personal Compass for 6 Core Values)

Personal Mastery- Knowing yourself

Achievement- Reaching Your Goals

Intimacy- Sharing yourself

Play & Creativity- Following Your Intuition

Search for Meaning- Spiritual Integrity

Compassion & Contribution

It's important at all times to know and understand what season of life that we are in. Often, we don't recognize why our lives are feeling uncomfortable and disorderly during certain stages.

**Becoming A Consciously Aligned Leader**

I strongly believe it is because we are not in flow with our seasonal alignment.

If you put on a January sweater in the middle of July and wonder why you are about to burst into flames, it's because you are not properly dressed for the season.

We get the same results when we don't make the proper shifts to become more aligned with a particular season of our life.

Again, it is important to know and understand your seasonal alignment. Exploring the six core values can always serve as a navigation tool for helping you determine the two to three areas that you might need to focus on during a certain phase. Of course, I always love to encourage individuals to make personal mastery one of their tops areas; however, I believe that it's all self-mastery at the end of the day.

**Becoming A Consciously Aligned Leader**

**Personal Mastery** from the six core values is about focusing on knowing yourself. We all reach a point where we know ourselves well enough to where we don't have to continue to work on ourselves as much so we spend time operating from our true sense of knowing.

**Achievement** consists of reaching your goals and proving yourself to yourself and not seeking the outside approval or validation from others. **Intimacy** is about sharing yourself with others in meaningful relationships through divine connectivity or sharing your gifts in a more profound way.

**Play & Creativity** consist of following your intuition enjoying and expressing yourself. As spiritually aligned leaders, we need to often step back from being a human doing to being a human being who enjoys fulfilling recreation.

**Becoming A Consciously Aligned Leader**

**Search for Meaning** is an adventure of exercising and demonstrating your spiritual integrity as you integrate yourself in your everyday affairs. **Compassion & Contribution** invites you to begin leaving a legacy by giving of yourself and your resources.

Another component that I created and use in the Life Aligned tele-class is what I call the *5 Cornerstones Stages of Cultivation*. In the early stages of building my coaching and consulting platform, I felt out of alignment with my endeavors. I was either trying to move too fast in one area that I needed to be still in or I was moving to slow in an area that I needed to be in motion.

As a result, I began to explore and assess my current navigation strategy for my next steps and that is what led me to create the five cornerstones to use for myself and my clients.

**Becoming A Consciously Aligned Leader**

During my tele-classes and/or private consulting sessions, I invited individuals to identify their top core focuses such as their business, education or a project because they might find that in more than one stage at a time. *The 5 Cornerstones Stages of Cultivation* is gardening your endeavors wisely.

It's only when we truly connect with our proper divine alignment, we connect with our purpose. Ecclesiastes 3:1-8 explains that there is a time and a season for everything this is why it is important to know the current season of life that we are in so that we are not tearing down something when we should be building it.

**Becoming A Consciously Aligned Leader**

### 5 Cornerstone Stages of Cultivation

Discovery/Preparation

Build/Development

Movement/Execution

Shift/Reinvention

State of Rest: Expectancy & Stillness

The first stage of **Discovery/Preparation** consists of the beginning framework for your endeavors. This process takes time, becoming more equip and focused exploration to come into the right alignment to move forward.

The second stage **Build/Development** is similar to the first stage, yet it allows you to begin to build, develop and course correct upon the blueprint and framework of your preparation and explorations. The third stage of cultivation is **Movement/Execution,** which encourages you to get into motion with the right inspired actions in divine timing that were strategies in the first two phases.

**Becoming A Consciously Aligned Leader**

Using the fourth and fifth stages of **Shift/Reinvention & the State of Rest,** which consist of **Expectancy & Stillness,** are the key cornerstones that can be integrated at any time during the first three stages. No matter what the endeavor is, making the proper adjustments or shifts to recreate is always critical in the first three stages.

Reinvention is often one of the stages that most leaders miss out on for experiencing a higher level or purpose and transformation. Often, they are not willing to try something new or reinvent themselves for the next phase.

The fifth stage of the State of Rest is about expecting and being still enough when you've done all that you can. There comes a time in the seed and harvest process that the ground must rest.

**Becoming A Consciously Aligned Leader**

We must allow this same process to be present in our experiences. At times, we have to pull back and allow Spirit to bring about the desired manifestations or speak to us about our next steps.

Applying these stages of cultivation within our personal, professional and spiritual lives will help us to move with divine alignment so that our journeys flow with more grace and ease as we pursue what we were destined to do.

A life aligned is a life divine, the correct alignment always provides you with the GOD Formula: Good-Orderly- Direction to know that your path is being infused with Spirit so that you can co-create and serve as your highest Self.

**Becoming A Consciously Aligned Leader**

## *Master the Art of Simplicity for Leaders*

On this journey of self-mastery, I've learned that mastering the art of simplicity is a very key component of operating from a holistic alignment framework. Primarily in the Western world, we have unfortunately learned how to master the art of "more, more, more," along with the art of "busy, busy, busy." There have been several products and processes created that make it very convenient for us to try to accomplish more.

Unfortunately, most think that if we have more simplified processes, this will allow us to be able to do more. Yes, this is true. Simplicity can allow us to leverage our time more effectively to accomplish more; however, here is the catch; more than likely we will abuse that privilege of having more rather than use our remaining time to do the things that really matter most.

**Becoming A Consciously Aligned Leader**

Often, we forget or neglect the important things like spending time with the ones you love, like family, covenant relationships, community, church or spending more time with God.

Do we even take the time to do something nice for ourselves to improve our overall well-being? The list could go on. I recall at one point in my business when I was doing the solo-preneur model, I would find ways to simplify my business goals only so that I could assure more time to work on other business-related projects. This was a vicious cycle of running on that human hamster wheel, which later assisted in the decline of my health.

As my health declined, I had to slow down and do less. After doing this, I saw greater results in my overall life, as I truly began to embrace the art of simplicity to live by the concept of "less is more."

### Becoming A Consciously Aligned Leader

Learning how to keep it simple and being consistent with the flow of mastering this area is what is really needed for leaders to connect more deeply into that inner knowing within. This helps to build a better relationship with the Spirit, God, ourselves and others.

Mastering the art of simplicity is all about simplifying your life so that you can focus on and be a part of the most important things in life. This is especially critical for us as leaders to embrace so that we don't live our lives in regret of wishing that we hadn't spent so much time and energy towards our roles in our jobs, ministry or community and not having the well-rounded or balanced lives that God designed for us.

So, I challenge you to simplify your lives so that you can enjoy and experience every good thing that this life affords you.

**Becoming A Consciously Aligned Leader**

Learning how to live and lead from this place of simplicity allows us to experience all of the fullness of life in very practical and meaningful ways.

We can live a better-quality life when we are more focused on the quality and not the quantity. The illusion of "more, more, more" and "busy, busy, busy" begins to shift so that we can enjoy more of the simple ways that life wants to gift us.

# *Leaders Should Bring Purpose to Everything*

One of the most talked about subjects these days besides the economy is centered around finding or knowing your purpose.

I recall participating in an Intuitive Coaching Now conference call with Visionary & Coach, Anya Sophia Mann, where on the call a woman expressed how she felt paralyzed by her current purpose. She expressed how at one phase in her life she had been called to serve her family. However, at the current time, she felt that she had been doing that for so long that she no longer knew what her purpose was anymore.

Anya, softly said to her, "This is your purpose, to bring purpose to everything that you do and your purpose will naturally unfold." After hearing this, the woman broke into tears of joy and freedom.

**Becoming A Consciously Aligned Leader**

This was also an eye-opener for me as well with my own journey and the work that I do with leaders. We get caught up spending a lot of time and energy focusing on what we should be doing right now or our next steps.

As leaders and people of great influence continue to move forward to overcome procrastination or prevent stagnation, it is important to continue to bring purpose to everything until our next levels of purpose unfold.

The power of purpose is in our every move. Our journey is to live on purpose and bring purpose to every aspect of our lives.

## *Conclusion*

In closing, remember that you are the change agent that you've been looking for. Now go forth and be that change in the world, because the world needs your example now more than ever before.

Our lives are not just for us, as leaders we are here to help evolve the whole of humanity; therefore, we must make every effort to be in true connection to ourselves and Source in order to be in alignment with our mission so that we can fulfill the divine plan for our lives.

# *Becoming A Consciously Aligned Leader*

# *Reflections & Planning Section*

# *Record Your Insights from The Reading*

*What steps will you take this week or this month to consciously make the proper shifts and alignments?*

## *More Notes:*

# *Record Your Insights from The Reading*

*What steps will you take this week or this month to consciously make the proper shifts and alignments?*

## *More Notes:*

# *Record Your Insights from The Reading*

*What steps will you take this week or this month to consciously make the proper shifts and alignments?*

*More Notes:*

## *Record Your Insights from The Reading*

*What steps will you take this week or this month to consciously make the proper shifts and alignments?*

*More Notes:*

## *Record Your Insights from The Reading*

*What steps will you take this week or this month to consciously make the proper shifts and alignments?*

## *More Notes:*

# *Record Your Insights from The Reading*

*What steps will you take this week or this month to consciously make the proper shifts and alignments?*

## *More Notes:*

# Write A Brief Summary About Your Conscious Planning Experience

# *Summary Continued:*

**Becoming A Consciously Aligned Leader**

**For More Resources**

*www.consciouscorporatestrategies.blogspot.com*

*www.amazon.com/author/alicianwaters*

**Or**

**To Book the Author**

**For Speaking Engagements**

**Email:** www.anwempires@gmail.com

**If you enjoyed this resource, please consider writing a review on Amazon.com**

**Thanks & Blessings!**

Becoming A Consciously Aligned Leader